In the
UPPER
ROOM

In the
UPPER
ROOM

A One-Act Play

by Lisa Soland

An All Original Play Publishing
Acting Edition

IN THE UPPER ROOM

Written by Lisa Soland
Copyright © 2004 by Lisa Soland

Published in 2024 by All Original Play Publishing
P.O. Box 32381
Knoxville, TN 37930
AllOriginalPlays@gmail.com

First Edition: March 2024
Printed in the United States of America
Graphic Design by All Original Play Publishing

Front and back cover photos by Stefan Holt

ISBN: 978-1-956218-32-9
Library of Congress Control Number: 2024903164

"Still, as of old,
Man by himself is priced.
For thirty pieces Judas sold
Himself, not Christ."

— *Mary Cholmondeley, Diana Tempest*

The history of
IN THE UPPER ROOM

Initially titled *The Lord's Last Supper*, this play was first produced on April 4, 2004, at Bethel Lutheran Church in Encino, California. Playwright Lisa Soland directed, Luise Strauss designed the costumes, and Andy Eichner composed the special music. The original cast, in order of appearance, was as follows: Brian Barnett played *Judas Iscariot*, Kevin Kruse played *James*, Andy Eichner played *John*, Chris Durmick played *Simon Peter*, Tim Mahoney played *Andrew*, Matt Smith played *Philip*, Dennis McClintock played *Nathanael*, Joe Russell played *Jesus*, Deryk Stilwell played *Thomas*, Stephen Sleezer played *Simon the Zealot*, Ken Burrows played *Judas not Iscariot*, Buzz Brown played *Matthew*, and Duane Judisch played *James the Less*.

The Lord's Last Supper was then produced at Lifehouse Church in Northridge, California, on May 16, 2004, with Stephen Barnett in the role of *Philip*, and then at The Atherton Baptist Homes in Alhambra, California, on June 26, 2004. Chip Chalmers played *Simon the Zealot*, Dan Pawlowski, *Andrew*, and Stephen Barnett, *Matthew*.

A second production was mounted two years later, on April 13, 2006, at Bethel Lutheran Church in Encino, California, for the Maundy Thursday church service. Auditions were held, and those cast were from a pool of professional actors living and working in the Los Angeles area. Lisa Soland directed, Theatre Encino produced, and Luise Strauss designed the costumes. The cast was as follows: Brian Barnett played *Judas Iscariot*, Jason Little played *James* and Justin Little played *John*, Todd Covert played *Simon Peter*, Terry Woodberry played Simon Peter's brother, *Andrew*, Devin Reeve was *Philip*, Alvin Lam was *Nathaniel*, Paul McDade played *Jesus*, Tommy Jeff as *Thomas*, Stephen Barnett as *Simon the Zealot*, Joszef Fahey played *Judas not Iscariot*, Carlo Monido played *Matthew*, and Deryk Stilwell was *James the Less*.

Then, two days later, on April 15, this second cast traveled to the Ventura Youth Correctional Facility in Camarillo, California. The cast and crew gained entrance into the co-ed prison and quickly restaged the play to suit the prison's protestant chapel. Eighty prisoners attended, both men and women between the ages of 14 and 24.

Buzz Brown, who organized the event, stated that this was the first time he had ever seen the prison sponsor a co-ed attended event. "With five years experience working with hundreds of wards, hundreds of times, this was the best behaved group I've ever seen. They were joyful when the play called for them to be, and respectful when the Word was given. There was no need for 15 staff officers. More attended simply to see the play. One switched his schedule, and one came in on her day off. Chaplain Sandy of Ventura Prison called Chaplain Bruce of Chino Prison to tell him what a wonderful performance it was and that he should look forward to it."

Carlo Monido, cast in the role of *Matthew*, attended Bethel's worship service on April 9, 2006, and shared his testimony with the congregation as a youth who had been in and out of prison until a Christian visited and ministered to him. That day, he committed his life to Jesus Christ, and when released, he never looked back.

On April 30, 2006, the play was performed twice in the Heman G. Stark Correctional Facility for Youth, California's most violent Juvenile Prison, while at its peak in population. The prison held wards as young as 12 years of age and was closed in 2010 due to persistent violence. Actors Duane Judisch, Mark Krcmaric, and Steven Watson joined the cast for these two productions. Luise Strauss designed costumes, and we again included Andy Eichner's original music.

CHINO YOUTH PRISON – APRIL 30, 2006
THE LORD'S LAST SUPPER

BRIAN BARNETT.................Judas Iscariot "the traitor"
CARLO MONIDO...Matthew
TODD MASON COVERT...........................Simon Peter
TERRY WOODBERRY.......................................Andrew
TOMMY JEFF...Thomas
MARK KRCMARIC............................Simon the Zealot
ALVIN LAM...Nathaniel
JASON LITTLE...James
JUSTIN LITTLE..John
PAUL McDADE...Jesus
DEVIN REEVE..Philip
DERYK STILWELL
        and DUANE JUDISCH...............James the Less
JAY PARKISON................................Judas not Iscariot

The 3rd Production
CAST IN ORDER OF APPEARANCE

This publication of the play *In The Upper Room* is the
revised script of the third production, which took place
in the Hub at West Park Baptist Church in Knoxville,
Tennessee, opening on April 12, 1999, and running for
three performances. Lisa Soland directed, Stefan Holt
designed the lights, and Charlene Bledsoe designed the
costumes.

Violinist...Kimberly Simpkins

Judas..Lily Kate Corley
Simon Peter...Trevor York
John...Christian Holt
James..Anna Brice
Andrew..Rachel Shamblin
Philip..Austin Percival
Nathanael..Genevieve Oliver
Jesus...Simeon Thress
Judas not Iscariot.................................Shawn Williams
Matthew...RedPaint Spilman
Thomas..Abby Shamblin
James the Less...James Holt
Simon the Zealot....................................Stephen Polson

CREW

Playwright / Director...................................Lisa Soland
Technical Director..Stefan Holt
Set Construction..Stefan Holt
Costume Designer.............................Charlene Bledsoe
Costume Construction............Charlene Bledsoe, Velma
Farnsworth, Kay Thomas & Alice Patton
Original Music.......................................Andrew Eichner
Photographer...Stefan Holt

DESCRIPTION

In The Upper Room brings to the theatre the events surrounding the Passover meal Jesus shared with his disciples the night before he was crucified. In this one-act drama, Jesus shares memorable lessons that include the washing of His follower's feet and the Parable of the Wheat and the Tares. The play concludes with an original song created from the words of Psalm 118, which is thought to be the Psalm the men sang that night before leaving for Gethsemane to pray.

This play is a one-act and is to be presented
with no intermission.

TIME: Approximately 33 A.D.

PLACE: In the Upper Room in Jerusalem, where Jesus spent his last night with the twelve disciples.

CHARACTERS

Simon Peter: The leader of the twelve disciples. Inquisitive, asks questions, loud, impulsive, speaks before he thinks. Brother to Andrew. Later, they crucified his wife first and made him watch, then crucified him.

John: Jesus named John and his older brother James "Sons of Thunder." They were a couple of hotheads, quick-tempered and selfish. They came from a prominent family—"Sons of Zebedee." John later became known as the "Apostle of Love." He was banished to the island of Patmos, where he died.

James: Named "Sons of Thunder" by Jesus, along with his younger brother John. Has an elevated sense of self. He was the first to be martyred for his faith by being stabbed with a sword by King Herod Agrippa I. *(Not King Herod Antipas, who killed John the Baptist and put Jesus on trial, but his nephew and successor.)*

Andrew: Andrew was the first disciple to be called by Jesus. He was fine with living in the shadow of his brother Simon Peter, whom he brought to Jesus. Martyred on a cross, shaped like an "X," and brought people to Jesus even as he hung there.

Philip: Leader of the second group of disciples. Arranged meals and the logistics. The "travel manager" for the group. Friends with Nathanael.

Stoned to death at Heliopolis, in Phrygia, due to his faith.

Nathanael: Philip's closest friend. Also known as "Bartholomew." Was martyred either by being tied up in a sack and thrown into the sea or crucified.

Matthew: Before taking up his cross and following Jesus, Matthew was a tax collector. Tax collectors were the most despised people of Israel, more so than occupying Roman soldiers. He was burned at the stake for his faith.

Thomas: Worrywart, negative, always looking on the dark side. Martyred for his faith by being stabbed with a spear.

James the Less: Possibly smaller in stature than the rest or younger or simply younger than the other James. Could be Jesus' cousin. He was either stoned, beaten, or crucified.

Simon the Zealot: An outlaw and member of the political sect. In normal circumstances, Simon the Zealot would have killed Matthew. Simon was killed for preaching the Gospel, but it is unknown how.

Judas not Iscariot: Called the "heart child" or "breast child" by the other disciples. Later, he took the Gospel north to Turkey and was clubbed to death for his faith.

Judas Iscariot: The traitor. All the other disciples were from Galilee, but Judas came from Keriothhezron, south of Judea. He held the purse and was the keeper of the money. Appeared devout but was a wicked man. Committed suicide after betraying Jesus by hanging himself, but died because the limb broke on the tree. He is a tragic character. He couldn't even choose the way he died.

Jesus: The Messiah. Calm, loving, and patient beyond belief. He knows truth because He is truth. Jesus is aware that this evening is the last He will have with His disciples. He continues to teach and guide them, fully aware of what is to come.

IN THE UPPER ROOM

SETTING: The play takes place in the Upper
            Room where Jesus spent his last night
            with the 12 disciples.

AT RISE: A single violinist stands downstage of
            thrust. She is dressed in black contem-
            porary clothing and plays an instru-
            mental version of "His Loving
            Kindness" on her violin. Near the end
            of the piece, she steps off the thrust and
            exits down the center aisle through the
            audience as Judas steps onto the stage.

JUDAS: *(Judas surveys the room. He is alone.)* "Meet
us in the upper room at sunset." I have grown
impatient with their perpetual lateness.
(Mocking their excuses.)
"Oh, but we had to heal the sick. We had to
raise the dead. We had to cast out demons."
*(He crosses downstage onto the thrust and
looks out over the city.)*
Oh, Jerusalem.
(Beat.)
Jesus entered the city with triumphant shouts
of "Hosanna," and they all laid down their
palm leaves before him. But alas, three years of
following this Rabbi and the shackles of Rome

remain, with Herod still as its King—not our beloved "Messiah."

(Angrily turns away.)

What a complete waste of my time!

(Back to the window.)

The chief priests and elders wait for my report, and then I shall hand him over to them.

(He experiences a momentary compassion, then continues.)

So, he claims to be the Son of God...

(He removes his sack of coins from his belt.)

Well then, surely, he can save himself from what is to come.

(He tosses the sack of coins into the air and catches it. Then turns upstage and tosses the sack again. He crosses to the front of the stage left of the table, then tosses the coins again.)

Sold for the price of a slave.

(He sits on the table.)

Not bad.

(He empties his sack of coins onto the table, then begins to count.)

Two, four, six, eight...

(John and James enter first, then Simon Peter, and Andrew in fast pursuit. They are in the middle of a heated dispute. Judas quickly returns the coins to his purse and tucks them around his belt.)

SIMON PETER: *(To James and John.)* You did what?!!!

JOHN: What's it to you, Simon?

SIMON PETER: It's everything to me. I'm one of you. We are all in this together.

JAMES: *(Sarcastically.)* Yeah, right.

JOHN: Since when?

SIMON PETER: If you're going to be asking for special thrones in Jesus' kingdom, we have a right to know about it.

JOHN: *(Confessing.)* It was our mother, all right? It was our mother who insisted.

SIMON PETER: Insisted? What are you, a couple of mama's boys?

ANDREW: And you call yourselves "Sons of Thunder."

JUDAS: *(Almost to himself.)* Well, now Jesus knows the truth of you.

SIMON PETER: *(Quickly to Judas.)* Jesus knows the truth of us all.

JAMES: At least we're willing to stand up for what we believe!

JOHN: And for what we deserve!

ANDREW: For what you deserve?!

SIMON PETER: If you're so deserving, what did Jesus say, John?

ANDREW: How did he respond to your request?

JOHN: *(Correcting him.)* Our mother's request.

ANDREW: Oh, yes—your "mother's request."

JOHN: *(Finding it difficult to admit.)* Well...

SIMON PETER: Please. Share with us what our Lord and Master said.

JAMES: *(Stepping in.)* Jesus told us that we had no idea what we were asking.

JOHN: *(Growing with pride.)* And then he asked us if we were able to drink of the same cup that he was about to drink.

ANDREW: The same cup?

JUDAS: What cup?

SIMON PETER: *(Quickly.)* What did you say?

JAMES: We said...

(Looking to John.)

JAMES and JOHN: *(With ignorant confidence.)* We were able.

SIMON PETER: *(Growing angrier, mocking them.)* You?! Oh yeah, a couple of hotheads helping our Lord run his kingdom? Sitting on his right and left?

(Angrily crosses to John, backing him off the thrust, stage left.)

What right do you have to ask for such a thing when I am obviously more deserving?

JOHN: *(Laughing.)* More deserving?!

JAMES: *(Laughing along with John.)* More deserving of what? Criticism?!

JOHN: *(Pretending to be Simon Peter.)* "Lord, if it is you, command me to come to you on the water."

JAMES: *(He jumps onto the stage, right of the table, and, pretending to be Jesus, joins in the mocking. He calls out to John with his hand outstretched.)*

Come.

(John mimes getting out of a boat with confidence, at first looking at James/"Jesus,"

then he looks down at the "water," and his legs begin to tremble.)

JAMES: *(Acting as if he is Jesus.)* Simon Peter, don't take your eyes off me. Trust. Look at me! Peter!

JOHN: *(As Simon Peter, with his eyes looking down, he begins to sink.)*

I can't do it. I'm afraid. Oh Lord, save me. I'm drowning!

SIMON PETER: *(Rushes John and pushes him to the ground, upstage left. In the fall, the actor's head makes it safely to the last of the sitting pillows, stage left of the table.)*

How long are you going to remind me of my shortcomings?

ANDREW: *(Casually.)* Yeah, knock it off, John. You're reminding him of his wife.

SIMON PETER: *(To John.)* I didn't see you jumping out of the boat. Jesus called out to all of us, and no one got out of the boat but me.

JAMES: *(Crosses to Simon Peter in an attempt to help John.)* Simon, let him go.

SIMON PETER: *(Pushes James away. Then to John, who is still pinned to the ground.)*

Courage is rare, my friend. I'd say that makes me the most deserving.

(Philip and Nathanael enter through the audience left onto the stage right carrying sacks of food.)

PHILIP: Fighting again, boys? How predictable.

JOHN: Get off. You're hurting me.

SIMON PETER: Oh, Mama's Boy is crying.

JAMES: *(Tries to come to John's aid again but to no avail.)* Get off of him, Peter.

NATHANAEL: *(Mocking them.)* "I'm the greatest. No, I'm the greatest."

JUDAS: *(Rises, crosses to Philip.)*
Where's my change?

PHILIP: You mean *our* change, don't you, Judas?

JUDAS: I'm the keeper of the purse. Hand it over.
(Philip hands Judas one piece of silver. Judas looks at the one piece, then up at Philip with distrust.)

JUDAS: That's it?

PHILIP: It was more than we expected.

JUDAS: What you mean is you purchased more than you expected. More than what we need. Again.

PHILIP: If you find it difficult to trust me...
(Grandly introduces Nathanael as one who tells the truth.)
Behold an Israelite in whom there is no deceit.

JUDAS: *(Asking Nathanael.)* All right, Nathanael—you tell me. What happened to all that money I put in your trust?

NATHANAEL: Judas, we're celebrating the Passover meal with Jesus, our friend and Messiah. This could be our last meal with him. And it may sound completely unimaginable to you, but we could care less about the money.

JUDAS: Once again, this man is the reason we spend what we don't have on things we don't need.
(He puts the coin into his money sack and

returns to sitting on the stage left of the table. Somewhat to self.)

I've grown tired of it.

JAMES: *(Trying to take hold of Simon Peter from behind.)*

Simon, I told you to let him go.

SIMON PETER: *(He pushes James to the ground while continuing to hold John.)*

I'm not letting him go till he admits that I am the greatest.

JAMES: Well, you're the boldest, that's for sure.

(Jesus enters with the rest of the disciples through the audience left and onto the downstage right of the stage.)

JESUS: *(Primarily to Simon Peter.)* The one who is the greatest among you must become like the youngest and the leader like the servant.

SIMON PETER: *(He quickly releases John.)*

Yes, of course. Forgive me, Jesus.

JESUS: It is only through complete humility that we are able to love completely, as our heavenly father loves us.

(Everyone listens.)

JESUS: *(Picks up the basin.)* Here by the door, the basin waits, yet not one of you accepted the task. *(Beat.)* Who is greater, the one who reclines at the table or the one who serves? The world will tell you it is the one who reclines at the table. But, I am among you as the one who serves.

(Crosses to stage right of thrust, sets basin down, removes his outer garment.)
Everyone who exalts himself will be humbled, and he who humbles himself will be exalted. *(He sits, then invites John to sit with him at the wash basin.)*
John.

JOHN: *(Sits, then quietly to Jesus.)* You want to wash my feet?!

JUDAS: *(To Simon Peter, Andrew, and James.)* Surely a slave's duty.

JESUS: *(Begins to wash John's feet.)*
Just as my Father has granted me a Kingdom, I grant you that you may eat and drink at my table in my kingdom, and you will sit on thrones, all of you, judging the twelve tribes of Israel.

SIMON PETER: *(Confirming this with Jesus.)*
All of us, then?

JOHN: That's what he said. What're you deaf?!

SIMON PETER: *(Angrily rushes John.)* I'm just making sure you heard him.

JESUS: *(Jesus finishing with John's feet.)* Simon Peter, son of Jonah...
(He nods for Simon Peter to sit with him.)
Join me.

SIMON PETER: *(Humbly, in disbelief.)* Lord, do you wash my feet?

JESUS: My heart is fixed upon you. This evening, my heart is fixed upon you all.

SIMON PETER: *(Prideful.)* But not my feet.

JESUS: What I do you do not understand now, but you will come to understand soon after.

(Everyone looks to Simon Peter. He hesitates.)

JAMES: *(Pushes Simon Peter hard from behind.)* Go ahead, Simon.

JOHN: *(Mocking him.)* Yeah. You can't drown in three inches of water.

(Simon Peter angrily runs toward John and grabs him once again.)

JESUS: *(Calmly stopping Simon Peter.)* Peter?

SIMON PETER: *(In disbelief.)* My Lord, you are the Christ. The son of the living God.

(Turns away in refusal.)

NEVER WILL YOU WASH MY FEET!

JESUS: If I do not wash you, you have no part with me.

SIMON PETER: *(Suddenly changing his stance, he quickly sits and removes his sandals.)* If that be so, Lord, then wash not only my feet but also my hands and my head.

(Pushes his hands into the wash bin.)

JESUS: *(Gently taking hold of Simon Peter's wrist.)* He who has bathed needs only to wash his feet but is completely clean, and you are clean, but not all of you.

JUDAS not ISCARIOT: *(Confused.)* Not all of us, Jesus?

JESUS: Not all of you are clean.

(Jesus looks to Judas, implying that he sits down next.)

Judas.

JUDAS: *(Crosses to Jesus, then stands above him, looking down.)*
Must you?

JESUS: *(Looking up.)* God opposes the proud but gives grace to the humble.
(Judas notices that everyone is looking at him, so he sits and allows Jesus to wash his feet, looking away. Jesus begins to tenderly and lovingly wash Judas' feet. Judas begins to watch Jesus and becomes transfixed by his actions.)

JESUS: I do not speak concerning all of you. I know well those whom I have chosen. But that the scripture may be fulfilled, "Even my close friend in whom I have trusted, who eats bread with me will lift up his heel against me."
(He dries Judas' feet, then stands and puts on his outer garment.)
I am telling you this now, before it takes place, that when it does take place, you may believe that I AM—he.

MATTHEW: We believe you, Lord. And we are faithful.

JESUS: Truly...
(Crosses to upstage center, downstage of table.)
...truly, I say to you, one of you will betray me.

SIMON PETER: One of US?
(They all look at each other. Simon Peter motions for John to ask Jesus who he means.)

JOHN: Lord, who is it?

ANDREW: *(Coming forward.)* Is it me?

JAMES: *(Coming forward.)* Lord? Me?

JAMES the LESS: *(Crossing in.)* Me?

SIMON PETER: If it's me, Lord, tell me, and I'll go away to keep it from happening.

THOMAS: *(With anxiety in his heart, he rises and steps on Judas' foot.)*
It's not me, is it? Please tell me it's not me.

JUDAS: Thomas, you're stepping on my foot!
(Judas pushes him away. Everyone turns to watch Judas and Thomas.)

THOMAS: *(Backing up further.)* Oh, I'm sorry. I didn't mean to, Judas.

JESUS: *(Whispered to John.)* It is he to whom I will give this piece of bread when I have dipped it.
(Dipping the bread into the olive oil, he then hands it to Judas.)
What you are going to do, do quickly.
(Judas exits quickly down the center aisle. The disciples are confused.)

(LIGHT CUE. Night has come.)

JESUS: *(Looking after Judas as he exits.)*
What you mean for evil, God will use for good.

SIMON PETER: *(Crosses down center, perplexed, watching Judas exit.)*
Where is he going?

PHILIP: We already have everything we need.

JESUS: *(Prays.)* I have guarded them, Father, and not one of them has been lost, except the son of destruction that the scripture might be fulfilled.

(He raises arms up to the heavens.)

Now is the Son of Man glorified, and God is glorified in him.

THOMAS: *(He crosses down center, thinking he may have offended Judas.)*

I uh... I stepped on his foot, but I told him I was sorry.

JESUS: *(Gently.)* Thomas, what Judas does, he does willingly.

THOMAS: All right, Jesus.

JESUS: *(Kisses Thomas' forehead, then turns upstage.)*

Please be seated. All of you.

(Everyone crosses upstage to sit at the table in the following order, stage right to stage left: Simon the Zealot, James the Less, Nathanael, Matthew, Andrew, Simon Peter, Jesus, John, James, Philip, Thomas and Judas not Iscariot. Simon Peter and Jesus share a moment downstage center. Then Simon Peter crosses upstage right of the table to sit.)

JESUS: *(Attempting to explain evil to them. He crosses upstage left.)*

The kingdom of heaven is like a man who sowed good seed in his field...

(Matthew quickly searches for his writing utensil and paper.)

SIMON PETER: *(As Simon Peter crosses behind the table, to Matthew, shocked.)*

What are you doing?!

MATTHEW: *(To Simon Peter.)* You're the one who told me I should be writing all this down.

SIMON PETER: Be still!

JESUS: Peter.

SIMON PETER: Forgive me.

JESUS: The kingdom of heaven is like a man who sowed good seed in his field, but while men slept, his enemy came and sowed tares among the wheat and went his way. But when the grain had sprouted and produced a crop, then the tares also appeared. So the servants of the owner came and said to him, "Sir, did you not sow good seed in your field? How, then, does it have tares?"
(Crosses upstage of table, a bit stage right.)
He said to them, "An enemy has done this." The servants said to him, "Do you want us then to go and gather them up?" But he said, "No, lest while you gather up the tares, you also uproot the wheat with them. Let both grow together until the harvest, and at the time of harvest, I will say to the reapers, "First gather together the tares and bind them in bundles to burn them, but gather the wheat into my barn."

THOMAS: What does it mean, Jesus?

JESUS: The Son of Man sows the good seed.

SIMON PETER: *(Explaining to Thomas.)* We're the good seed, Thomas.

ANDREW: The field is the world, isn't it?

JESUS: Yes, Andrew. *(Beat.)* The good seeds are the sons of the kingdom, but the tares are the sons of the wicked one.

JOHN: Satan.

JESUS: Yes, John.

THOMAS: *(Rises, crosses to Jesus, then takes his left arm.)* And you allow them to grow up side by side. All around us.
(Jesus nods.)

JOHN: Why? Why, Jesus?
(John takes Jesus' right hand.)

JESUS: *(To John.)* So that your love for me will grow and become complete.

JOHN: For love, then?

JESUS: Yes, for love.
(John takes Jesus' right hand and places it on his upstage cheek.)

THOMAS: What's the harvest?

JESUS: The end of the age. *(Jesus sits.)* In the end of times, the Son of Man will send out His angels, and they will gather out of His kingdom all things that offend and those who practice lawlessness, and they will cast them into the furnace of fire. There will be great wailing and gnashing of teeth. Then the righteous will shine forth as the sun in the kingdom of their Father.

SIMON PETER: *(To Thomas.)* That's us. We're the righteous.

JESUS: And the humble.

SIMON PETER: *(Smiles.)* And the very humble.

JOHN: So, you will come for us then, Jesus.

JESUS: Yes, I will come for you. I promise.

(To the others.)

I promise you all.

(They are quiet.)

PHILIP: All this talk of wheat is making me hungry. Can we eat now, please?

(Most reach for the food plates.)

JESUS: *(Stopping them.)* Remember this! The one who rejects you, rejects me. And the one who rejects me, rejects him who sent me.

PHILIP: Lord?

JESUS: *(Smiling.)* Yes, Philip. We can begin.

(They reach for the food and begin to put it on their plates, not yet eating. Waiting for the prayer.)

SIMON PETER: *(Puts his hand on Jesus' shoulder, reassuring him.)*

We'll remember, Jesus.

(Philip hands Jesus the loaf of bread.)

JESUS: *(Jesus kneels, then takes the loaf of bread and blesses it, praying upward toward the heavens.)*

Father, bless this food that it may strengthen our bodies so that we may accomplish the work which you have set before us.

(He eats a piece of the bread, then breaks the rest of the loaf in half.)

Take, eat; this is my body, given for you. Do this always in remembrance of me.

(Jesus passes half to the disciples sitting on his left and half to those on his right, then waits for all to have their portion. He then takes a cup, fills it with wine, then again lifts it to the heavens and blesses it.)

Father, bless this wine that we may drink from it and be sanctified in Truth. Your word is truth.

(He drinks from the cup.)

Drink from it, all of you, for this is My blood of the covenant, which is poured out for many for forgiveness of sins.

(Jesus passes the cup to his right and waits till each has their portion. Simon the Zealot stands and humbly returns the cup to Jesus.)

JESUS: *(Primarily to Simon the Zealot.)*

But I say to you, Simon, I will not drink of this fruit of the vine from now on until that day when I drink it new with you in My Father's kingdom.

SIMON the ZEALOT: I look forward to it, Lord.

(He returns to sitting at stage right of table. Jesus then passes the glass of wine to the rest of the disciples on his left and waits for them all to drink of the cup. They are now all bonded as one.)

JESUS: *(Sits on a small stool behind the table; he looks at them with favor.)*

Little children, I am with you only a little while longer.

SIMON PETER: Little while longer?

(They all listen intently.)

JESUS: You will seek me, but where I am going, you cannot come. So, a new commandment I give to you—that you love one another, even as I have loved you...

JOHN: Love one another?

(They all lightly laugh at the thought.)

JESUS: Yes. That you also love one another. By this all men will know that you are My disciples if you have love for one another.

ANDREW: You're joking.

NATHANAEL: We can't even get along.

JUDAS not ISCARIOT: *(Rises.)* Couldn't you just command us to get along?

(Everyone laughs.)

JESUS: *(Smiling.)* A day is coming soon, when that will change.

(He holds out his arms as if on the cross.)

Greater love has no one than this, that someone lay down his life for his friends. You shall love your neighbor as yourselves.

SIMON PETER: How is that even possible?

JOHN: Tell us of these changes so we can prepare for them.

JESUS: Where I am going, you cannot follow me now, but you will follow later.

SIMON PETER: Lord, why can't I follow you right now? I will lay down my life for you.

JESUS: Will you lay down your life for me, Simon?

SIMON PETER: Yes, Lord. Of this alone I am certain.

JESUS: Truly, truly I say to you, the rooster will not crow until you have denied me three times.

SIMON PETER: *(Severely crushed.)* No, not me, Lord. Not me.

JESUS: And where I go, you know, and the way you know.

THOMAS: *(Rises up to his knees.)* Lord, we do not know where you are going, and how can we possibly know the way?

JESUS: I am the way, the truth, and the life. No one comes to the Father except through me. *(Beat.)* If you had known me, you would have known my Father also, and from now on, you know him and have seen him.

PHILIP: *(With pride.)* Lord, show us the Father, and it is sufficient for us.

JOHN: *(To Philip, amazed at his stupidity.)* Show us the Father? What do you think he's been doing for the past three years?

JESUS: Have I been with you so long, Philip, and yet you have not known me? He who has seen me has seen the Father, so how is it that you can say, "Show us the Father?"

JOHN: Idiot.

JESUS: *(Lovingly correcting John.)* John.

JOHN: *(Quickly.)* Sorry.

JESUS: *(To Philip.)* Do you not believe that I am in the Father and the Father is in me?

PHILIP: *(Shaking his head, trying hard to understand.)*

It's not that I don't believe, Jesus. I do. It's just that I struggle.

JESUS: The words I speak to you, I do not speak on my own authority, but the Father who dwells in me; he does the work. Believe me that I am in the Father, and the Father is in me, or else... believe me for the sake of the works themselves.

THOMAS: *(Rises to knees and leans over the end of the table toward Jesus.)*
You have given us many works to remove all our doubt, Lord.

JESUS: And yet you still doubt, don't you, Thomas?

THOMAS: *(Shamefully.)* Yes, Lord.

JESUS: You still doubt.

THOMAS: I cannot seem to keep myself from doubting.

JESUS: *(To everyone.)* Truly, truly, I say to you, he who believes in me, the works that I do, he will do also, and greater works than these he will do.

(The following three lines overlap.)

SIMON PETER: *(With hope and disbelief.)* Greater?

ANDREW: Greater works?

SIMON PETER: Greater than you?!

(Everyone responds verbally with disbelief.)

JESUS: Because I go to the Father. I am your advocate, and I speak to him on your behalf. Whatever you ask in my name, that I will do so that the Father may be glorified in the Son.
(To Simon Peter.)

If you ask me anything in my name, Peter, I will do it.

SIMON PETER: *(With grand swagger-like support, he rises, rallying the troops.)*

We will ask everything in your name! Right? EVERYTHING!

(The following three lines overlap while everyone joins in, showing their support.)

JOHN: Yes, Lord.

JAMES: We will.

MATTHEW: Most assuredly.

JESUS: If you love me, you will keep my commandments.

SIMON PETER.:We love you, Lord.

(He sits.)

(The following three lines overlap while everyone joins in.)

THOMAS: *(Rises.)* Yes, we do—

JOHN: *(Rises.)* We love you—

JUDAS not ISCARIOT: *(Rises.)* We love you with our whole hearts.

(Everyone reassures Jesus of their great love for him.)

JESUS: *(Taking a moment to receive their love.)*

After a little while, the world will no longer see me, but you will see me. Because I live, you will live also.

JAMES the LESS: *(To Simon the Zealot.)*

What is he saying?

SIMON the ZEALOT: Jesus, we are a little confused.

JESUS: *(Explaining.)* He who has my commandments and keeps them is the one who loves me. That is how I know you have love for me. This is how I feel your love. And he who loves me will be loved by my Father, and I will love him and will reveal myself to him.

JUDAS not ISCARIOT: What then has happened that you are going to disclose yourself to us and not to the world?

JESUS: These things I have spoken to you while abiding with you. But the Helper, the Holy Spirit, who the Father will send in my name... The Holy Spirit will teach you everything. Even how to love.

MATTHEW: *(Up on his knees.)* This Holy Spirit will teach us all things?

JESUS: Yes, Matthew. He will lead you from within, and bring to your remembrance all that I have said to you.

MATTHEW: So, I'll be able to write it all down then, after this Holy Spirit comes?

JESUS: *(Exactly.)* Yes. That's right.

JOHN: Me too, Jesus? Can I write it all down too?
(Everyone laughs.)

JESUS: You too, John. You will be doing a lot of writing.
(To Matthew and John.)
You will remember, and you two will write all that I have said and done for the millions of believers to come.

JUDAS not ISCARIOT: Future believers who won't be

able to know you as we have known you?

JESUS: Yes.

MATTHEW: From a ruthless tax collector to a
historian. That is the most difficult thing to
believe.

JESUS: Don't doubt. Believe every piece of what I have
told you. And, above all, dear friends—do not
be afraid.

SIMON PETER: Lord, you're going away. My heart is
deeply troubled by this news.

ANDREW: How can we not be afraid?

JOHN: Yes, Lord.
(Places his head on Jesus' left shoulder.)

SIMON the ZEALOT: We are surrounded by our
enemies. Those who hate us.
*(Everyone verbally agrees with Simon Peter
and Andrew, expressing their fear and deep
sadness.)*

JESUS: Do not be afraid—in any place, with any
person, for any reason. Because my peace I will
leave with you; my peace I give to you; not as
the world gives but as I give to you. As my
followers in this world, you will have
tribulation, yes, most certainly.
(Faces front.)
But take heart, I have overcome the world.

SIMON PETER: *(Troubled.)* My Lord, what will we
do?

JESUS: Do not let your heart be troubled.

ANDREW: But we've given up everything for you—

SIMON PETER: Our livelihood. Our fishing—

JESUS: *(To Simon Peter.)* You will become great fishers OF MEN.

SIMON PETER: Of men?

JESUS: Are not your neighbors more important than fish? Are not their souls more important than *eating* fish?

(Everyone agrees with Jesus.)

JESUS: Soon, I will be lifted up from the earth and will draw all people to myself. And you will be my witnesses both in Jerusalem and in all Judea and Samaria and even to the most remote areas of the earth.

PHILIP: *We're* going to do this?

NATHANAEL: But we're just ordinary people.

JAMES the LESS: *(Rising.)* Small people.

(Everyone laughs.)

SIMON the ZEALOT: *(Pulls James the Less into his side and razzes him playfully.)* Little James.

(Everyone laughs.)

JESUS: You will be given everything you need. The moment you step out in faith, the courage will appear. Even for you, Little James.

(Everyone laughs.)

JOHN: It's difficult for us to imagine doing anything without you, Jesus.

(Everyone expresses their concern.)

JESUS: Trust in me. I said that I will return to you.

(Joyously.)

If you loved me, you would be so joyful, every one of you, because I am going to the Father, and the Father is greater than I.

THOMAS: *(Sarcastically.)* "Oh, rejoice! He's leaving us. Halleluiah." Is that what you want us to say? Lord, I cannot keep the sorrow from pouring in upon me.

SIMON PETER: We are all deeply troubled by what you say.

(The following three lines overlap while everyone else joins in.)

THOMAS: Don't leave us, Lord.

PHILIP: Why do you have to go?

ANDREW: What will we do without you?

(Everyone passionately agrees.)

JESUS: Believe in God; believe also in me. In my father's house, there are many rooms. If it were not so, would I have told you that I go to prepare a place for you? And if I go and prepare a place for you, I will come again and will take you to myself, that where I am, you may be also. *(He rises.)* I have told you before it happens so that *when* it happens, you may believe and then give witness to all that you have seen. Your witness will be more powerful than you will know. So, do not lean on your own understanding. Trust in me with your whole being.

SIMON PETER: *(Stands and tries with all his heart to convince Jesus.)*

Jesus, I love you with my whole being. I will lay my life down for you. I will. I promise.

JESUS: Yes, I know your heart, Peter.

JOHN: *(Standing.)* We all will, Jesus.

JAMES: We will be there for you.

JESUS: I know.

SIMON PETER: All that we say is in earnest. Why don't you believe us?

(With loving kindness and wisdom, Jesus places his hand on Simon Peter's face and looks into his eyes and heart. Simon Peter recognizes a bit of truth in Jesus' eyes and is deeply saddened by his own sinful human nature. Simon Peter places his head on Jesus' chest, and Jesus lovingly embraces him.)

JESUS: *(To everyone.)* I will not speak much more with you, for the ruler of this world is coming, and he has nothing in me, but so the world may know that I love the Father, I do exactly as the Father commands me, which now requires a great deal of praying. Rise, my friends.

(He takes John's hand, who is on his right.)

Let us go from here and pray.

(Everyone rises and crosses to be in front of the table. Jesus begins to sing a hymn, and everyone joins in—Psalm 118.1-4 and then 118.22-29. This is the hymn of thanksgiving for the deliverance from enemies. It is thought that this was the actual hymn sung by Jesus and His disciples that night at the conclusion

of the Passover dinner. The sheet music follows.)

JESUS: GIVE THANKS TO THE LORD, FOR HE IS GOOD, FOR HIS LOVINGKINDNESS IS EVERLASTING. OH, LET ISRAEL SAY...

EVERYONE: HIS LOVINGKINDNESS IS EVERLASTING.

JESUS: OH, LET THOSE WHO FEAR THE LORD SAY...

EVERYONE: HIS LOVINGKINDNESS IS EVERLASTING. THE STONE WHICH THE BUILDERS REJECTED HAS BECOME THE CHIEF CORNER STONE. THIS IS THE LORD'S DOING; IT IS MARVELOUS IN OUR EYES.

(The group crosses onto the thrust.)

THIS IS THE DAY WHICH THE LORD HAS MADE; LET US REJOICE AND BE GLAD IN IT. OH, LORD, DO SAVE, WE BESEECH YOU; O LORD, WE BESEECH YOU; DO SEND PROSPERITY!

(The group slowly forms a united circle with arms about each other.)

BLESSED IS THE ONE WHO COMES IN THE NAME OF THE LORD. WE HAVE BLESSED YOU FROM THE HOUSE OF THE LORD. THE LORD IS GOD, AND HE HAS GIVEN US LIGHT; BIND THE FESTIVAL SACRIFICE WITH CORDS TO THE HORNS OF THE ALTER. YOU ARE MY GOD, AND I GIVE

THANKS TO YOU. YOU ARE MY GOD, I
EXTOL YOU.
JESUS: GIVE THANKS TO THE LORD, FOR HE IS
GOOD.
EVERYONE: FOR HIS LOVINGKINDNESS IS
EVERYLASTING.
(Everyone steps away, then looks back to Jesus.)
SIMON PETER: To Gethsemane, then?
JESUS: Yes. To Gethsemane.
(Everyone exits through the center aisle in silence as the lights fade out.)

END OF PLAY

HIS LOVING KINDNESS

Lisa Soland (adapted from Psalm 118)   Andrew Eichner

RUBATO, sung in plain-chant style

GIVE THANKS TO THE LORD, FOR HE IS GOOD;

FOR HIS LO-VING-KIND - NESS__ IS__ E - VER - LA - STING.

OH LET I-SRAEL SAY... HIS LO-VING-KIND - NESS__ IS__ E - VER

LA - STING. OH LET THOSE WHO FEAR THE LORD__ SAY...

HIS__ LO-VING-KIND - NESS__ IS__ E - VER - LA - STING. THE

STONE WHICH THE BUIL-DERS RE-JEC - TED__ HAS BE - COME THE

CHIEF COR - NER STONE. THIS IS THE LORD'S DO - ING;

IT IS MARV' LOUS IN OUR EYES. THIS IS THE DAY WHICH THE

LORD HAS MADE; LET US RE-JOICE AND BE GLAD IN IT.

2

31 OH LORD, DO SAVE, WE BE - SEECH YOU; O

36 LORD, WE BE - SEECH YOU; DO SEND PRO - SPE - RI - TY!

40 BLESSED IS THE ONE WHO COMES IN THE NAME OF THE LORD. WE HAVE

43 BLESSED YOU FROM THE HOUSE OF THE LORD. THE LORD IS

47 GOD, AND HE HAS GI-VEN US LIGHT; BIND THE FE - STI - VAL

51 SAC - RI - FICE WITH CORDS TO THE HORNS OF THE AL - TAR.

54 YOU ARE MY GOD, AND I GIVE THANKS TO YOU. YOU ARE MY GOD, I EX -

57 TOL YOU. GIVE THANKS TO THE LORD, FOR HE IS GOOD.

60 FOR HIS LO-VING-KIND - NESS___ IS___ E - VER - LA - STING.

PROPERTIES

Various plates, dishes, and pitchers of the first century time period.

COSTUMES

Thirteen, first-century tunics, some have head dressings, belts, and purses.

SET

Three separate long and short tables, able to sit four people behind each of them. Place one downstage center and the other two slightly overlapping the downstage center table, just upstage of it. Four tall white pillars stand split, two upstage and two downstage. Pillows for the actors to sit on can be placed upstage of the table and at the table's ends.

The second tour and cast of *The Lord's Last Supper*,
outside the prison in Southern California, 2006.
Cameras were not allowed inside.

Christian Holt played the role of John in the third
production and third cast of *In the Upper Room*, 2019.
(Photo by Stefan Holt)

The role of Jesus played by Simeon Thress in
In the Upper Room, 2019. (Photo by Stefan Holt)

Trevor York as Simon Peter in CedarBrook Outreach's
production of *In the Upper Room*, 2019.
(Photo by Stefan Holt)

What they're saying about
SERGEANT YORK: THE PLAY

"It's simply a wonderful play."
– *Deborah York, Executive Director of the Sergeant York Patriotic Foundation and great-granddaughter of Alvin York*

"*Sergeant York: The Play* is... a powerful statement on the nature of war and the power of faith."
– *Peter Colley, playwright/screenwriter/librettist*

"Fantastic play!! A job well done!!!"
– *Colonel Gerald York, grandson of Alvin York*

"I thoroughly recommend *Sergeant York: The Play* for any organization seeking an inspirational, wholesome tale of a true American hero."
– *Burt Rosen, President and CEO of Knox Area Rescue Ministries Knoxville*

"Soland has devoted her significant abilities to share the story of Alvin York's deep personal faith and commitment to Jesus Christ."
– *Sam Polson, Lead Pastor of West Park Baptist Church*

What they're saying about
30 SHORT PLAYS
FOR PASSIONATE ACTORS...

"Lisa Soland has here assembled a wonderful collection of short plays. If you're a passionate actor, a teacher or a director looking for a play to do, you won't find a better place to start looking than this book."
— Lawrence Harbison, Senior Editor, Smith and Kraus
& Applause Theatre & Cinema Books

**"Lisa Soland's amazing collection of
30 excellent, sooo entertaining short plays
is a must for any would-be playwright,
actor or acting group!"**
— *Tom Sawyer, novelist, playwright, screenwriter*

**"This collection of plays is as varied and eclectic
as the human mind itself. they are funny,
dramatic, poignant, shocking, outrageous,
satirical, imaginative... It's a must-have for
writers of short plays and a great resource for
theatres that produce them."**
— *Peter Colley, playwright, screenwriter, librettist*

What they're saying about
BORN TWICE...

The material for *Born Twice* was developed in an Acting/ Writing Workshop led and directed by Lisa Soland. The play is the result of interviews conducted by the original participants, and consists of six true stories of people coming to accept Jesus Christ as their Lord and Savior.

"Nothing is more compelling than the personal witness of a life changed by the power of God's love. I highly recommend *Born Twice* to all who are looking for answers about faith and for those who have already come to faith in Christ but want to know Him more deeply. I am certain that *Born Twice* will inspire all through these amazing stories of new life."

– Sam Polson, Lead Pastor of West Park Baptist Church

www.ingramcontent.com/pod-product-compliance
Lightning Source LLC
Chambersburg PA
CBHW070946120626
46546CB00004B/1584

* 9 7 8 1 9 5 6 2 1 8 3 2 9 *